Paris, 1925

Also in this series

POETRY

Selected Poems

Adam / Adán (1916)
Square Horizon / Horizon carré (1917)
Equatorial & other poems (1917-18)
Arctic Poems / Poemas árticos (1918)
Skyquake / Temblor de cielo (1931)
Citizen of Oblivion / El ciudadano del olvido (1941)
Seeing and Touching / Ver y palpar (1941)
Last Poems (1948)
Uncollected Poems

PROSE

El Cid / Mío Cid Campeador (1928)
Cagliostro (1934)
Three Immense Novellas / Tres inmensas novelas (with Hans Arp, 1935)

Manifestos (1925)
Adverse Winds / Vientos contrarios (1926)

Vicente Huidobro

Paris, 1925
Ordinary Autumn
    &*   *All of Sudden*

Automne régulier
    &   Tout à coup

*Translated from French and Spanish
by Tony Frazer*

Shearsman Books

First published in the United Kingdom in 2020 by
Shearsman Books
PO Box 4239
Swindon
SN3 9FN

Shearsman Books Ltd Registered Office
30–31 St. James Place, Mangotsfield, Bristol BS16 9JB
(this address not for correspondence)

www.shearsman.com

ISBN 978-1-84861-693-6

Translation copyright © Tony Frazer, 2020.

The right of Tony Frazer to be identified as the translator
of this work has been asserted by him in accordance with the
Copyrights, Designs and Patents Act of 1988.
All rights reserved.

Automne régulier was originally published in Paris in 1925 by
Librairie de France. (Although the cover is dated 1926, other evidence
indicates that the book actually appeared in late 1925.)

Tout à coup was originally published in Paris in 1925
by Éditions Sans Pareil.

The French texts here are based on the first editions, and on
the versions printed in the critical edition of the author's
Obra poética (Paris: ALLCA XX, 2003). The Spanish versions are based
on those printed in the *Obra poética*. Further textual
information may be found in the Notes, starting on p.156.

*I am grateful to Timothy Adès for a suggestion which
solved a problem in the translation of 'Le matelote'.*

This book has been set in Le Monde Livre, with
section titles and poem titles in Requiem Fine.

Vicente Huidobro in 1925

Huidobro had arrived in Europe in late 1916 and promptly made a name for himself in vanguard circles in Paris, mixing with the leaders of the new movement in poetry (Apollinaire, Jacob, Reverdy, Tzara), befriending many of the following wave (Cocteau, Cendrars among the French, Gerardo Diego, Juan Larrea and others in Spain), mixing with the most forward-thinking artists (Picasso, Gris, Picabia, Arp, Delaunay, Lipchitz) and composers (above all, Edgard Varèse who set Huidobro's words to music). In a bewildering period of 24 months – the calendar years 1917-18 – he published two full collections, *Horizon carré* [Square Horizon, in French] and *Poemas árticos* [Arctic Poems, in Spanish], together with four chapbooks: *Ecuatorial* [Equatorial] and *El espejo de agua* [The Water Mirror] – both in Spanish, the latter being a new edition of a book that had previously appeared in Buenos Aires in 1916 – *Hallali* and *Tour Eiffel* [Hallali and Eiffel Tower], both in French.

In the aftermath of the war, Huidobro calmed down a little, although he remained busy writing, publishing poems in magazines, editing magazines, writing polemics and manifestos and turning his hand to prose and to treatments for silent films. He published a short selected poems in French in 1921, *Saisons choisies* [Selected Seasons], a volume which brought into French some poems that had only previously seen the light of day in Spanish, but which otherwise might be regarded as being a place-holder until the author was ready to bring out something new. The book also included a manifesto, 'La création pure' [Pure Creation]. In 1921 he also travelled throughout Europe giving readings and lectures.

1925 was to see the next explosion of activity, reflecting the odd fact that on several occasions during his career, Huidobro was to publish several books at more or less the same time. In 1925, two books of poems in French appeared, *Automne régulier* and *Tout à coup*, along with a volume of manifestos (*Manifestes* – already translated in this series). The following year, when the author was back in his native Chile, there followed a volume of essays and aphorisms, *Vientos contrarios* [Adverse Winds]. This pattern was to repeat itself in 1931, when the masterpieces *Altazor* and *Temblor de cielo* [Skyquake] were published in Madrid, and again in 1941, when two large poetry collections, *El ciudadano del olvido* [The Citizen of Oblivion] and *Ver y palpar* [Seeing and Touching], appeared in Santiago.

In the two French-language volumes collected here, which have generally attracted little attention since their original publication, we see the author's direction of literary travel after that initial explosive period in the final years of the Great War. Unsurprisingly, one of the books (*Automne régulier*) demonstrates some influence from the Dada group – Huidobro was close to Tristan Tzara, for one, and had been elected one of Dada's "Presidents" – while the other (*Tout à coup*) has a decided whiff of surrealism and automatic writing about it, notwithstanding Huidobro's imprecations against the latter in his manifestos and his often uneasy public relationship with André Breton.

Huidobro did not like to be thought of as a follower, which is no doubt one reason why he kept starting new magazines and issuing polemics against his perceived enemies and competitors. The fact is, of course, that Huidobro had swallowed vanguard Paris whole after his arrival. His work changed dramatically in character, and one can see the obvious influences of Apollinaire and Reverdy upon his early Parisian work. He became something of a touchstone in Madrid, where the poets were unfamiliar with the latest Parisian developments, and Huidobro thus acted as a conduit between forward-looking Paris and (by comparison) rather backward Spain and Latin America. It is a fact that he would have hated to have said about him, but his poetry only starts to look really *different* in the mid-1920s, by which time the various influences had been fully digested. (This is not to belittle the poetry in the earlier books, which I greatly admire, but simply a recognition of certain fundamental truths…) These two French books demonstrate possible ways forward, but in the end represent roads not taken, and are in turn nothing like *Altazor* or *Temblor de cielo*, nor anything like some of the superb poems in the two 1941 collections, most of the contents of which were written between the mid-1920s and the mid-1930s.

So what is going on in the two books reprinted here? Well, first of all, literary Cubism – *le dernier cri* in 1918 – has subsided, and the much-vaunted Creationism (effectively Huidobro's own personal movement, despite his claims for its broader "membership") has also fallen by the wayside, although some critics have held that *Altazor* itself is a Creationist poem, perhaps because the author seems to have started it in 1918, and the book itself places its origin date in 1919. In any event, the label still gets bandied about, as if the label is more important than the poems that carry it. I don't believe that it is. Huidobro was good at self-publicity, at marketing, and many of the things that he did, and said, were to gain attention for himself; Creationism is best regarded as a marketing ploy, and the results of it, in poetic form, are strikingly similar to contemporary work by French poets such as Huidobro's erstwhile friend Reverdy. And there's nothing wrong with that; it reflects what was in the air, so to speak.

The first thing to strike the reader of *Automne régulier*, at least one who is familiar with the earlier works in either French *or* Spanish, is the sudden reappearance, after several years, of rhyme. The rhymes are however decidedly odd, and show the clear influence of Dada, whose adherents relished nonsense rhymes. Those readers who have no French will have to take this on trust, as I have mostly avoided rhymes in the translations except where they turn up naturally. The syntax of the English versions *generally* follows that of the French, where I can manage it without sounding too arch, and the occasionally peculiar line-endings should give one enough of an idea of the absurdities generated by the French rhyme schemes. Take the title poem, for instance:

Laissons la place aux matelots   [Let's make way for the sailors
Viens regarder dans mes îlots   Come and look in my islets]

The meanings here are less important than the oddity of rhyming *matelots* and *îlots*. Not to mention the glorious couplet in the final piece, 'Poème':

Je te dis que tu es belle
Comme une chambre d'hôtel

                      [*Literally*:   I tell you you're beautiful
                                          As a hotel room]

or, as translated here:

                                           I tell you you're a belle
                                           Like a room in this hotel.

There are some holdovers from the experimental work of 1917-18, in so far as the poet still often employs spatial schemes on the page (known as *field composition* in more recent times), although there is less resort to words floating free, and capitalisation of words, approaches that owed much to poets such as Apollinaire, but also to those Cubist paintings that employed floating pieces of text, or newspaper cut-outs. However, lines have generally become longer, although probably more so in the poems from the latter part of the date-range applied to the book (1918-1922). The poems start to be *thicker*, more padded out, than those in the period we might describe as the earlier high vanguard phase of Huidobro's writing. My theory is that one method of composition here was to come up with a couple of initial lines, or perhaps just the rhymes themselves, and then generate the rest of the poem from these starting fragments, although there is no way I can prove this. Thus, the interesting thing for me is the text that arises from what appears to be the Dadaist *chance operation* represented by the rhymes.

Tout à coup is a rather different book. Unlike its twin, none of the contents had previously been published. While *Automne* comes over as playful in a typically Dadaist way, something else is going on in this volume, and the texts are also all left-adjusted, lacking any attempts at a more exotic *mise-en-page*. Having railed in his manifestos against the "parlour-game" of automatic writing, here in line one of the first poem, we see: *Les deux ou trois charmes des escaliers du hasard sont incontestables* (The two or three charms of the stairways of chance are indisputable), the French *hasard* echoing through from Spanish *azar* (*chance*, or *luck*, which, in Spanish – if pronounced in the Chilean manner – is an almost exact homophone of the French word). And, of course, the book's title may well be a clue, an allusion perhaps to the rapidity of the collection's composition.

The poems have more *syntax* than was the case with Huidobro's earlier work; the progress of the language is mostly predictable, but the word choices are positively disruptive within that syntax, as one would expect from surrealist procedures; added to this are some wild rhymes of the kind we see in *Automne régulier*. The poems make little sense in any conventional way but they are certainly enjoyable to read, even if they do represent something of an experimental dead-end. It's curious that, on the one hand, the author was railing against Surrealism in his manifestos while on the other apparently using some of its mechanisms as a way of moving his own work forward. The prose-poetry of *Temblor de cielo* (Skyquake, written 1929, published 1931) shows clearly how Surrealist notions had seeped into the author's bones, as do many of the more *composed* poems from the same era, which were only to be collected in 1941.

I confess that I initially under-rated both of these books and, while I still feel that they represent an artistic blind alley, they remain fascinating documents worthy of attention today when one is trying to get a handle on the work of this protean talent. The two books deserve better than to be forgotten – neither have had much attention in France since their appearance and they have likewise been mostly ignored by students of the Latin-American avant-garde. There have been some Spanish translations over the years and the works were of course reprinted in the three collected editions of Huidobro's work (two Chilean editions of the *Complete Works*, in 1954 and 1966, and one *Poetic Works* in 2003), and also in the bilingual *Obras poéticas en francés* (Poetic Works in French, edited by Waldo Rojas, Santiago: Editorial Universitaria, 1999).

It should be noted that both first editions were poorly typeset, although it is perfectly clear how the poems should be lineated. I have corrected here such typographical errors[1] as exist in the original books, and have compared the first editions with the critical texts published in the 2003 *Obra poética*. While mostly impeccable as regards the Spanish texts, the latter is however never totally secure when dealing with French, and I have had to exercise my own judgement on occasion. Anyone who wishes to see the first editions can download free versions in PDF form from the Biblioteca Nacional de Chile. Further details on the texts, and my editorial approach, may be found in the Notes at the end of this volume, starting on p. 156.

Tony Frazer
April 2020

---

[1] One example may suffice here to indicate the kind of problems one can encounter. The title of the poem 'La Matelote' (see p. 60) was printed in the first edition as 'La Matelotte', and Huidobro – not to mention his occasionally erratic typesetters – often made this kind of spelling error when writing in French. This spelling was recognised as incorrect by Waldo Rojas (*Obras poéticas en francés,* 1999) , but he went on to assume that 'matelotte'/'matelote' actually meant "female sailor", by extrapolation from "matelot", and thus translated it into Spanish as 'La marinera'. By contrast, *I* assume, together with Cedomil Goic (*Obra poética*, 2003), that what was actually intended was 'matelote', "hornpipe" in English, a sailor's dance. In a text where reality is hard to find, however, such multiple meanings could well be part of the game.

CONTENTS

AUTOMNE RÉGULIER / ORDINARY AUTUMN

14	Automne régulier / Ordinary Autumn	15
18	Hiver à boire / Winter for Drinking	19
22	Relativité du printemps / Relativity of Spring	23
24	Été en sourdine / Silent Summer	25
28	Clef des saisons / Key to the Seasons	29
30	Femme / Woman	31
32	Globe-trotter / Globetrotter	33
36	Ombres chinoises / Shadow Puppets	37
42	Affiche / Poster	43
44	Charbon / Coal	45
46	Poème funéraire / Funeral Poem	47
48	Océan ou dancing / Ocean or Dancing	49
52	Poète / Poet	53
54	Honni soit qui mal y danse / Shame on Those Who Dance Badly	55
56	Mer mer / Sea Sea	57
58	Film / Film	59
60	La matelote / The Hornpipe	61
64	Ya vas hatchou / Ya vas khachu	65
66	Poème / Poem	67

Appendix: Spanish Versions

70	Estío en sordina / Silent Summer	71
74	Tarde / Evening	75
76	Cabellera / Hair	77
78	Poema funerario / Funeral Poem	79
80	Océano o dancing / Ocean or Dancing	81

TOUT À COUP / ALL OF A SUDDEN

86	I—XXXII	87

Appendix: Spanish Versions

152	XV	153
154	XXII	155

Notes   156

AUTOMNE RÉGULIER

(1918-1922)

«Le monde attend toujours son Poète»
EMERSON

ORDINARY AUTUMN

(1918-1922)

"...the world seems always waiting for its poet..."
EMERSON

AUTOMNE RÉGULIER

La lune tourne en vain

Dans ma main
La nuit et le jour
Se sont rencontrés
Et l'angle ouvert mieux qu'une bouche
Avale mes pensées

La lune moulin à vent
Tourne tourne tourne en vain
Le paysage au fond des âges
Et l'étang dans sa cage

En vain tu cherches
Arbre d'automne
Il n'y a plus d'oiseaux
                            Il n'y a plus d'oiseaux
En regardant sur les vallées
On voit partout des sons de cloches fanés
Le jour est plein mes mains aussi

A l'autre bout s'en sont allés
Les pas sans bruit

C'EST L'AUTOMNE DES CLOCHERS

Je ne sais plus de blonde ou brune
Laissons la place aux matelots
Viens regarder dans mes îlots
La nature morte du clair de lune
Avec l'assiette au bord de l'eau
Et la rose s'effeuillant sur l'oiseau qui chante
À minuit quarante

ORDINARY AUTUMN

The moon turns in vain

In my hand
Night and day
Have met one another
And the open angle wider than a mouth
Swallows my thoughts

The windmill moon
Turns turns turns in vain
The landscape throughout the ages
And the pond in its cage

In vain you search
Autumn tree
There are no more birds
                        There are no more birds
When looking out over the dales
We see everywhere the sounds of withered bells
The day is full   my hands too

At the other end steps
Receded without a sound

IT IS THE AUTUMN OF THE BELFRIES

I no longer recognise blonde or brunette
Let's make way for the sailors
Come and look in my islets
The still life of moonlight
With the plate at the water's edge
And the rose shedding petals onto the bird singing
At forty minutes after midnight

Oublie-moi
     Petit astre caché
C'est l'heure où j'embaume ma forêt
          Oublie-moi

Pilote sans navire et sans loi

Au fond de mes yeux
Chantera toujours le poète noyé

Forget about me
                        Little hidden star
It's time for me to anoint my forest
                                        Forget about me

Pilot with no ship and no law

In the depths of my eyes
The drowned poet will always be singing

HIVER À BOIRE

L'hiver est arrivé à l'appel de quelqu'un
Et les regards émigrent vers les chaleurs connues
Ce soir le vent traîne ses écharpes de vent
Tissez mes oiseaux chéris un toit de chants sur les avenues

Entendez-vous pétiller l'arc-en-ciel mouillé
Sous le poids des oiseaux il s'est plié

L'amertume a peur des intempéries
Mais il nous reste un peu de cendre du couchant
Hirondelles de ma poitrine comme vous faites mal
Secouant toujours ce silence végétal

Séductions d'antichambre en degré d'eau-de-vie
Éloignons de suite la voiture des neiges
Je bois lentement tes regards aux justes calories

Le salon se gonfle de la vapeur des bouches
De la lampe pendent les regards gelés
Et il y a des mouches
Sur les soupirs pétrifiés

Les yeux sont pleins d'un liquide voyageur
Et chaque œil a un parfum spécial
Le silence est une plante qui pousse à l'intérieur
Si le cœur garde son chauffage égal

Dehors approche la voiture des neiges
Portant son thermomètre d'outre-tombe
Et je m'endors au bruit du piano lunaire
Quand on tord les nuages et la pluie tombe

WINTER FOR DRINKING

Winter has arrived at someone's call
And eyes migrate towards known sources of warmth
Tonight the wind is dragging its wind scarves
You my beloved birds weave a roof of songs along the avenues

Do you hear the damp rainbow fizzling
It's bent under the weight of birds

Bitterness has a fear of bad weather
But we still have a few ashes left over from sunset
You swallows in my chest how painful you are
Always shaking that herbal silence

Seductions in the antechamber by strength of brandy
Let's move the car out of the snow right now
Slowly I drink in your glances efficient in calories

The living room swells with steam from mouths
From the lamp hang frozen glances
And there are flies
On petrified sighs

The eyes are filled with a homing liquid
And each eye has its own special scent
Silence is a plant that grows inside
If the heart keeps its heating steady

Outside the car approaches out of the snow
Wearing its thermometer from beyond the tomb
And I fall asleep at the sound of the lunar piano
When clouds are twisted and rain falls in the gloom

Tombe
Neige au goût d'univers
Tombe
Neige qui sent la haute mer

Tombe
Neige parfaite des violons
Tombe
La neige sur les papillons

Tombe
Neige en flocons d'odeurs
La neige en tube inconsistant

Tombe
Neige au pas de fleur
Il neige de la neige sur tous les coins du temps

Semence de sons de cloches
Sur les naufrages plus lointains
Réchauffez vos soupirs dans les poches
Car le ciel peigne ses nuages anciens
Suivant les gestes de nos mains

Larmes astrologiques sur nos misères
Et sur la tête du patriarche gardien du froid
Le ciel blanchit notre atmosphère
Parmi les paroles glacées à moitié chemin

Maintenant que le patriarche s'est endormi
La neige glisse glisse
                            glisse
De sa barbe polie

Falling
Snow with a universal taste
Falling
Snow with a smell of the open sea

Falling
Snow perfect for violins
Falling
Snow on butterflies

Falling
Snow in scented flakes
Snow in an inconsistent tube

Falling
Snow at a leisurely pace
It snows snow in all corners of time

Seed of pealing bells
On the farthest shipwrecks
Warm up your sighs in your pockets
For the sky combs its ancient clouds
Aping the movements of our hands

Astrological tears on our miseries
And on the patriarch's head guardian of the cold
The sky whitens our atmosphere
Amongst half-frozen words

Now that the patriarch has fallen asleep
The snow slides slides
                            slides
Off his polished beard

RELATIVITÉ DU PRINTEMPS

On ne peut rien faire contre les soirs de Mai
Quelquefois la nuit dans les mains se défait
Et je sais que tes yeux sont le fond de la nuit

A huit heures du matin toutes les feuilles sont nées
Au lieu de tant d'étoiles nous en aurons des fruits

Quand on s'en va on ferme le paysage
Et personne n'a soigné les moutons de la plage

Le Printemps est relatif comme l'arc-en-ciel
Il pourrait aussi bien être une ombrelle
Une ombrelle sur un soupir à midi

Le soleil est éteint par la pluie

Ombrelle de la montagne ou peut-être des îles
Printemps relatif arc de triomphe sur mes cils
Tout est calme à droite et dans notre chemin
La colombe est tiède comme un coussin

Le printemps maritime
L'océan tout vert au mois de Mai
L'océan est toujours notre jardin intime
Et les vagues poussent comme des fougeraies

Je veux cette vague de l'horizon
Seul laurier pour mon front

Au fond de mon miroir l'univers se défait
On ne peut rien faire contre le soir qui naît

RELATIVITY OF SPRING

There's nothing to be done about evenings in May
Sometimes the night in one's hands starts to fray
And I know your eyes are deep as the night

At eight in the morning all the leaves were born
In place of so many stars we will have fruit

When we leave we close the countryside
And no one tended sheep by the seaside

Spring is relative like the rainbow
It might as well be a parasol
A parasol over a sigh at noon

The sun is put out by the rain

Parasol from the mountains or maybe the islands
Relative Spring triumphal arch over my eyelashes
Everything is quiet to the right and on our path
The dove is warm as a cushion

Coastal Spring
The ocean all green in the month of May
The ocean is still our private garden
And the waves grow like ferns

I want that wave on the horizon
The only laurel for my brow

In the depths of my mirror the universe comes apart
There's nothing to be done about evening being born

ÉTÉ EN SOURDINE

L'été tout d'un coup sur le trottoir d'en face
Du côté de l'ombre le vent passe

Nous sommes assis autour d'une voix
Un oiseau de chaleur se pose sur ton doigt
Tandis que les pêches se gonflent sourdement

L'oiseau becquette les nuages
Où les pluies silencieuses vont en voyage

La vendange des mois et les raisins du jour
Si le pressoir est loin on y arrive toujours
Et le troupeau de nuages qui fuit
Suit lentement les chemins de l'air

Le ciel
        le ciel
                ma bergerie

Je crie à la bergère
Rentre ton troupeau de lits d'hôpital
Il est bien tard dans ton pays natal

Mes jours s'en vont
Ferme à clef l'horizon
L'horizon à l'horizon se lasse
Et ma tête blanchit de moutons qui passent

L'heure mouillée s'allonge et puis revient
Tout ce qui existe part du creux de tes mains

Vendange des années

SILENT SUMMER

Summer all of a sudden on the opposite kerb
On the shaded side the wind passes through

We are seated around a voice
A heat bird alights on your finger
While the peaches swell silently

The bird pecks at the clouds
Where silent rains set off on a journey

The harvest of months and the grapes of day
If the wine press is far away you can still get there
And the flock of clouds fleeing
Slowly follows paths in the air

The sky
        the sky
                my sheepfold

I cry out to the shepherdess
Bring back your flock of hospital beds
It's quite late in your native land

My days go on their way
Close the horizon lock and key
The horizon on the horizon is getting weary
And my head is whitened by passing sheep

The damp hour lengthens and then returns
All that exists begins in the palms of your hands

Harvest of years

                    Les nuages vont au pressoir
Il faut laver le ciel qui devient trop noir
Trop noir trop noir trop noir

La nuit s'échappe de mon armoire

La nuit
        La lune a traversé sans faire du bruit

                        The clouds head for the wine press
The sky that is getting too dark meeds to be washed
Too dark too dark too dark

Night escapes from my wardrobe

At night
      The moon passed without making a sound

CLEF DES SAISONS

Je possède la clef de l'automne
De ma poitrine naissent les feuilles jaunes
Et un soir je dois pleurer tous les ruisseaux

A quoi bon suivre l'oiseau du tout d'un coup
Le jour meurt dans tes joues

Ne pense à rien
Entre les feuilles il y a la nuit qui vient
Il y a une heure qui s'enfuit
Et l'horloge est agreste
Il y a la pluie à gauche et l'aéroplane à l'est

Il y a une musique de harpe qui a frisé tes cheveux
Et au fond du ciel un arbre en feu
Pour dormir la terre s'épanche
Cachée à nos regards sous quelques branches

La pensée moins végétale de la journée
Dans mon doigt s'est posée
Pour attendre ensemble l'aube acide
Toutes les chansons tombèrent de la mésange en vol

Séduisons l'oiseau qui se vide
Et qui meuble de chants les ardoises et le sol

KEY TO THE SEASONS

I possess the key to Autumn
From my chest sprout yellow leaves
And one evening I must weep out all the streams

Why follow the bird all of a sudden
The day is dying on your cheeks

Don't think about anything
There amongst the leaves is the approaching night
There is an hour fleeing
And the clock is rustic
There's rain to the left and an aeroplane to the east

There is harp music that has put curls in your hair
And deep in the sky a tree on fire
So as to sleep the earth gushes out
Hidden from view under a few branches

The least herbal thought of daytime
Has perched on my finger
So we can wait together for the acid dawn
All the songs fell from the bluetit flying past

Let's seduce the leaking bird
Which endows the roof tiles and the soil with songs

FEMME

Dans mon étoile native
Elle était toute seule
                           Loin
               Au milieu de la forêt captive
               Le bateau nouveau-né
               Ne sait plus retourner

On entendait un poème
Qui jaillit du couchant

        Et tout l'univers tombait dans l'étang
Au centre de la terre

                MOI

J'ai eu peur de sa voix

             Cette aile unique de ma poitrine
                 Ne veut plus battre
Pourtant les soirs au cinéma
J'aurais si bien joué
Toute la musique de ses cheveux
Mais
                 La barque qui attend
                 Au milieu des oiseaux

Ces voiles
         Tous les nuages se gonflent
C'est le vent de ma flûte qui m'emporte cette fois

Les mouettes volent autour de mon chapeau
Et je m'éloigne sur le fil de ta voix

WOMAN

On my native star
She was all alone
                                      Far away
                        In the midst of the captive forest
                        The newborn boat
                        Can no longer return

A poem could be heard
Gushing from the sunset

        And the whole universe fell into the pond
At the centre of the earth

                      I MYSELF

I was afraid of its voice

                This solitary wing on my chest
                    Won't beat any more
Yet on movie nights
I would have played
All the music from her hair so well
But
                        The boat which waits
                        Amongst the birds

These sails
        All the clouds swell up
It's the wind from my flute that carries me away this time

Seagulls fly around my hat
And I walk away on the threads of your voice

GLOBE-TROTTER

Ton regard bleu
                ton regard bleu
Tant de vagues tant de rochers
                Où va-t-on?
Dans quel port laisserai-je ma chanson?

Le vent fait tourner les étoiles
Et le navire s'éloigne
Sur ton regard qui tremble

Par ici ont passé
Mes vers et mes années

Dans cette mer douce prairie
Broutée tous les printemps
Dans cette mer ont fait naufrage
Toutes mes barques fleuries

Matelot du couchant
                    regardons les girouettes
Je n'irai jamais aux plages sans mouettes

Toujours debout
Matelot au fond du ciel
Avec les bras ouverts dans la proue

La fumée de ta pipe a gonflé les nuages
Et tout le ciel sent ton tabac

            Regarde là-bas
            Matelot triste
            D'être un Christ
            Sur les mâts

GLOBETROTTER

Your blue gaze
                your blue gaze
So many waves so many rocks
                Where are we going?
In which port will I leave my song?

The wind makes the stars turn
And the ship is leaving
Under your trembling gaze

Over here my verses
And my years have passed

In this gentle sea meadow
Grazed every Spring
All my flowered boats
Have foundered in this sea

Sunset sailor
                let's watch the weather vanes
I will never go to beaches that have no gulls

Still standing
Sailor deep in the sky
With arms open at the prow

The smoke from your pipe inflated the clouds
And all the heavens smell of your tobacco

                Look over there
                Sailor sad
                At being a Christ
                On the mast

Levons les bras
Vers le ciel qui naît de l'eau
Vers cette aube oubliée par les oiseaux

Le vent fait tourner les étoiles
Et je suis ses yeux poissons natales
Entre les doigts un peu d'azur
Écume de mer sur les chaussures

Le point de l'horizon est mon chapeau
Et sur toutes les plages
Ma cravate au vent est un drapeau

Globe-trotter
Je suis loin de moi-même
Au fond de ce brouillard je me souviens
(Un souvenir qui luit comme une lanterne
Orange dans la main)

J'étais au collège j'étais interne
Et je passais l'été
Au bord de tes yeux bleus

Let's raise our arms
To the sky born of water
Towards this dawn forgotten by birds

The wind makes the stars turn
And I am their eyes native fish
Between my fingers a little blue
Sea foam on my shoes

The point on the horizon is my hat
And on every beach
My necktie in the wind is a flag

Globetrotter
I am far away from myself
Deep in this fog I remember
(A memory that shines like a lantern
Orange in my hand)

I was in high school I was a boarder
And I spent the summer
On the edge of your blue eyes

OMBRES CHINOISES

La colombe est tachée de charbon
Mais nous avons encore la pureté de l'avion
Cette hostie bien-aimée levée sur tous les monts

L'Avion
           L'Avion

Ce morceau de terre détaché de la terre
Fait le printemps de l'air

Nos ciseaux ont coupé les navires qui s'en iront
Et pour les suivre j'ai mes mains pleines de papillons

Détaché de moi-même je me regarde en face
Ce serait ma lune ou bien ma glace
Et je me dis bonjour
En ôtant l'abat-jour

Pourquoi donc cacher l'étoile fidèle
J'ai la clef des planètes qui tournent lentement
Je le sais bien
Les yeux ennemis s'ouvrent tout le temps
Et si tu pars je t'appelle

L'alouette du téléphone dort sur la ficelle

J'aime plus que tout les villes cosmogoniques
Les colliers de lanternes antiques

Les soirs de pluie toutes les villes sont Venise
Toutes les tours imitent celle de Pise

SHADOW PUPPETS

The dove is stained with charcoal
But we still have the purity of the aeroplane
This beloved host raised above all the mountains

The Aeroplane
                        The Aeroplane

This piece of land detached from the earth
Makes Spring out of air

Our scissors have cut out the departing ships
And so as to follow them I have my hands full of butterflies

Split into two I look myself in the face
This would be my moon or even my mirror
And I greet myself
By raising the lampshade

So why hide the faithful star
I have the key to slowly turning planets
I know it well
Enemy eyes are watchful all the time
And if you leave I will call to you

The telephone lark is sleeping on the wire

More than all the cosmogonic cities I love
Necklaces made of antique lanterns

On rainy evenings all cities are Venice
All towers imitate the one in Pisa

J'aime les rues ruisselantes dans la brume native
Pleines de jours et d'autos à la dérive

Cette descente de lampes vers l'abîme plus tiède

Émigration polaire
C'est simple
         et tout au fond ces fleurs d'itinéraire
Font une constellation familière

La ville est sans surprises
L'air du printemps sort de ma poche
Dans le clocher les heures sont prises
Et le vent qui passe tourne à gauche

Jazz band d'oiseaux
Dans le jet d'eau

Tu danses
         Tu chantes
Le lac du clair de lune est au degré cinquante

Le nègre rit comme un piano
Il a la bouche
Pleine de touches

La lune est son banjo
Et dans la gorge il étrangle un oiseau

Le jazz band d'outre-mer est venu sous les mouettes
Et les vagues ont pris un rythme nouveau
Tremblement de guitare noyé dans les flots
Le troupeau de la mer a suivi notre houlette

Je n'aime pas l'Amérique
Je n'aime plus le Printemps électrique
Où chaque feuille en s'ouvrant faisait un bruit mécanique

I like rain-slicked streets in the native mist
Full of days and cars adrift

These lamps descending towards the warmer abyss

Polar emigration
It's simple
        and right at the bottom these travel flowers
Make a familiar constellation

The city has no surprises
The Spring air emerges from my pocket
In the belfry hours are captured
And the passing wind turns left

Jazz band of birds
In the water jet

You dance
        You sing
The moonlit lake is at fifty degrees

The negro laughs like a piano
He has a mouth
Full of keys

The moon is his banjo
And in his throat he's strangling a bird

The jazz band from overseas arrived beneath seagulls
And the waves have taken on a new rhythm
Quivering guitar drowned in the waves
The herd from the sea followed our lead

I don't like America
I don't like the electric Spring any more
Where each leaf made a mechanical noise when opening

Le nègre a son nombril au diapason
Mais la colombe est tachée de charbon
Et nos aéros n'ont pas encore une chanson
Il faut qu'ils chantent nos avions
Comme des flûtes tournées vers l'avenir

Il est le nœud du ciel aujourd'hui
Demain il sera vieux aussi
Et il chantera peut-être pour mourir

Il n'y a plus de nouveaux sons
Toutes les âmes s'en vont

Mon âme telle qu'Ulysse est lente à revenir

The negro has his navel in tune
But the dove is stained with charcoal
And none of our balloons have a song yet
Our aircraft   they have to sing
Like flutes facing the future

It is the knot of heaven today
Tomorrow it too will be old
And perhaps it will sing so it can die

There are no more new sounds
All the souls leave

Just like Ulysses my soul is slow to return

AFFICHE

Dans tes cheveux il y a une musique
Sous l'étoile quotidienne ma guitare unique

Ta chevelure pleuvait sur la campagne

Celui qui a perdu le chemin
A l'autre rive tombera dans l'espace

   Astre natal
   Cet oiseau dans la gorge me fait mal
   Et ma vie
   Derrière moi reste endormie

En bas du soir
Une voix qui crie
ÊTRE AVEUGLE À MIDI

   Je regarde mon toit
   Douce mer pleine d'aventures
   Et le collier de tes larmes
   Rouillé dans ma poitrine

Fumée du vide
Chevelure fidèle de mon navire

   Ces fils qui montent à l'horizon
   Sont les cordes oubliées de mon violon

POSTER

In your hair there is a kind of music
Under the mundane star my guitar is unique

Your hair rained over the countryside

That man who lost his way
On the other bank will fall into space

        Native star
        This bird in my throat is hurting me
        And my life
        Behind me remains asleep

Down below in the evening
A voice that shouts
TO BE BLIND AT NOON

        I look at my roof
        Placid sea full of adventures
        And the necklace of your tears
        Corroded on my chest

Smoke from the void
Faithful hair from my ship

        These threads rising to the horizon
        Are the forgotten strings of my violin

CHARBON

Son regard est un animal qui court court au milieu du pôle
Il allume l'incendie de forêts lointaines
Quand la nuit tombe tous les ruisseaux s'envolent
Et les bois du ciel changent la position des plaines

Le rossignol norvégien
Aime les charbons des yeux les jours de froid
Et nous parle tendrement
Il a un petit accent

Que me dit-il   Une tasse de lait
Pour les rescapés
Il a mis des touches dans le vent
Et il porte son deuil
A l'heure du bain sur les plages de l'œil

COAL

His gaze is an animal running running at the centre of the Pole
It sets distant forests ablaze
When night falls all the streams fly away
And the woods in the sky switch position with the plains

The Norwegian nightingale
Loves the eye's coals on cold days
And speaks to us tenderly
It has a slight accent

What does it tell me   A cup of milk
For the survivors
It has put touches to the wind
And it is in mourning
At bath time on the eye's beaches

POÈME FUNÉRAIRE
À Guillaume Apollinaire

L'oiseau de luxe a changé d'étoile
Appareillez sous la tempête des larmes
Votre cercueil à voile
Où s'éloigne l'instrument du charme

Dans les végétations des souvenirs
Les heures autour de nous font les voyages

Il va vite
        Il va vite poussé par les soupirs
La mer est chargée de naufrages
Et j'ai drapé la mer pour son passage

C'est ainsi le voyage primordial et sans billet
Le voyage instructif et secret
Dans les couloirs du vent

Les nuages s'écartent afin qu'il puisse passer
Et les étoiles s'allument pour montrer le chemin

Que cherches-tu dans les poches de ta veste
As-tu perdu la clef

Au milieu de ce bourdonnement céleste
Tu rencontres partout tes heures vieillies
Le vent est noir et il y a des stalactites dans ma voix

Dis-moi Guillaume
As-tu perdu la clef de l'infini

Une étoile impatiente allait dire qu'elle a froid

La pluie aiguisée commence à coudre la nuit

FUNERAL POEM
for Guillaume Apollinaire

The luxurious bird has changed stars
Rig your coffin's sails
Beneath the storm of tears
Where the enchanted instrument heads into the distance

In the flora of memories
The hours all around us go off on journeys

It moves quickly
                It moves quickly driven by sighs
The sea is full of wrecks
And I have draped the sea for its passage

That's how it is the vital but unticketed journey
The informative and secret journey
Along the wind's corridors

The clouds drift apart so it can pass
And the stars light up to show the way

What are looking for in your jacket pockets
Have you lost your key

In the midst of this celestial humming
Everywhere you meet your aged hours
The wind is black and there are stalactites in my voice

Tell me Guillaume
Have you lost the key to infinity

An impatient star was about to say it was cold

The sharp rain begins stitching the night

OCÉAN OU DANCING

Jazz band de l'Océan
Ce bateau danse mal et je perds le pas

Là-bas
        Le ciel et la mer se joignent
Tant pis si le ciel est bleu et le poisson se noie

Au bord de la mer le port se balance
Partout où je vais je garde cette cadence

J'embrasse tes mains qui dénouent les jours
Tes petites mains s'en vont toujours
Comme les bateaux amour chevelure de l'horizon

Le port recule
        dernière chanson

Ma gorge refroidit
           tes doigts aussi

Et tout au loin tu tiens ton cœur
Comme on tient une fleur
Mais le rythme de ta poitrine est dans la mer
Et les vagues sont chaudes du rythme de ton cœur

Amour amour du jeune nageur
Joueur de harpe entre les vagues

        L'horizon se défait

Écume qui naît
        écume qui meurt
Écume qui danse sur les heures

OCEAN OR DANCING

Jazz band of the Ocean
This boat dances badly and I miss my step

Over there
                The sky and the sea come together
Too bad if the sky is blue and the fish is drowning

At the seaside the port is swaying
Everywhere I go I keep up this pace

I kiss your hands that unravel the days
Your little hands always leave
Like boats like love like the horizon's hair

The port recedes
                final song

My throat is chilled
                    your fingers too

And far away you're holding your heart
As if it were a flower
But the rhythm of your breast is in the sea
And the waves are warm with the rhythm of your heart

Love love of the young swimmer
Harp player amongst the waves

        The horizon is coming apart

Sea foam being born
                    sea foam dying
Sea foam dancing on the hours

La mer est fatiguée d'agiter ses mouchoirs
Aux navires qui s'éloignent

La nuit habituelle fait son devoir
Lune tasse de lait
                Nos étoiles se soignent
L'océan du sud entre deux arbres
Tant de couronnes dans l'eau
L'océan bien-aimé sous le marbre

Tu boiras goutte à goutte le clair de lune tout chaud

Cette fumée qui monte des flots
Traîne lentement son bateau
Poème du soir jouet d'enfant

Les navires s'éloignent comme tes mains

The sea is weary of waving its handkerchiefs
At departing ships

The usual night does its duty
Moon cup of milk
                        Our stars are healing
The southern ocean between two trees
So many crowns in the water
The beloved ocean beneath the marble

Drop by drop you will drink the piping hot moonlight

This smoke rising from the waves
Slowly drags its boat along
Evening poem child's toy

Ships move away like your hands

POÈTE

Poète poète sans sortilège
Trois jours après le naufrage
Moulin moulin de neige
L'épaule est lourde de nuages

Vous êtes tous des robinets
Votre cœur saigne par le nez
Mais les oiseaux sont des buffets trop pleins
Les oiseaux dans le ciel sont plus chauds que les mains

Tais-toi rossignol au fond de la vie
Je suis le seul chanteur d'aujourd'hui
Je vous répète mille fois
Que mon épaule est lourde de nuages
Mais j'ai la flûte officielle du chérubin sauvage

POET

Poet poet with no enchantment
Three days after the sinking
Mill mill snowmill
Shoulders weighed down with clouds

You are all faucets
Your heart bleeds through your nose
But the birds are over-filled buffets
The birds in the sky are warmer than your hands

Keep quiet nightingale at the core of life
I am the only present-day singer
I have told you a thousand times
That my shoulders are weighed down with clouds
But I have the wild cherub's official flute

HONNI SOIT
QUI MAL Y DANSE

Regardez Madame la lune décroît
Et les fruits se gonflent tous à la fois

Farine d'aveugle et rayons de lune
Le magasin vend son bouquet d'œufs
Les nuits obéissantes à l'appel des brunes[1]
Quand les planètes tournent dans les yeux du bœuf

Madame votre œil en bouteille de mer
Laisse échapper les parfums de mes vers

Les voyageurs venaient sur un fil de fer
Ils venaient en équilibre tels que viennent les mots
Les mots à mi-hauteur parcourent l'univers
Et souvent sont mangés par les oiseaux

Il ne me reste rien dansez la capucine
Et buvons le couchant comme une grenadine

---

[1] It is possible that this word should be "brumes" (fogs / mists), but there is no clear evidence.

SHAME UPON THOSE WHO DANCE BADLY

Look Madam the moon is waning
And all at once fruits are swelling

Blind man's flour and moonbeams
The shop sells its bouquet of eggs
Nights obedient to the call of brunettes
As planets turn in the ox's eyes

Madam your eye in a bottle at sea
Lets the scent of my verses escape

The travellers came by wire
They came balanced just the way words arrive
Words travel the universe at half height
And are often eaten by birds

There's nothing left for me dance the capucine*
And let's drink the sunset like a grenadine

The title is a play on 'Honi soit qui mal y pense', an old French maxim, which is also the motto of Britain's chivalric Order of the Garter (dating from the 14th century), and which translates roughly as "Shame on whoever thinks badly of it", or "Evil be to him who evil thinks". 'Honni' is the modern French spelling.

* The capucine (lit. nasturtium) is a traditional French children's dance, in which the accompanying song begins "Dansons la capucine" (Let's dance the capucine).

MER MER

La mer
Et le voilier plus joli qu'une guitare

L'écume les vagues
Blanchisseuses au hasard

Le bateau de retour
En passant par ici ferme le jour

Adieu aux vagues qui tonnent
Adieu à l'heure qui sonne
Adieu aux mâts sans feuille tout l'automne

N'oubliez pas
Le navire qui se noie
Et qui laisse pour tout marbre un cercle expansif
J'aime ce signe amical

Phare compréhensif
Bien plus que l'œil boréal
Amour de la beauté
Et de la fleur navale

Je laisse mon rameau à tes pieds
Femme debout sur le dernier rocher
Avec les yeux ouverts pour les bateaux en danger

SEA SEA

The sea
And the sailing boat prettier than a guitar

Foam from the waves
Random washerwomen

The boat returning
On the way here closes the day

Farewell to the thundering waves
Farewell to the ringing hour
Farewell to the masts leafless all Autumn long

Don't forget
The ship foundering
And leaving a widening circle for any marble
I like this friendly sign

Comprehensive beacon
Far more than the northern eye
Love of beauty
And of the naval flower

I leave my branch at your feet
Woman standing on the last rock
Her eyes open for boats in danger

FILM

Cow-boy dans les regards et le Far-West
Charme l'oiseau d'un geste
Cow-boy de l'œil mon véhicule
Promesse de fleuve au premier acte
Cow-boy qui pousse au crépuscule
Et veut sauter sur le public intact

Il siffle les Niagara et il arrête son bruit
Le rideau tombe bien plus belle cataracte
Alors sur la fleur et le phare qui s'acclimate
Il y a un soupir qui fait la nuit
Et là-haut Vénus épingle à cravate

Jeune fille souriant sur l'univers
Elle sera reine de tous les rêves de mer
J'aime ton chapeau dans la prairie
Et le berger qui garde son troupeau de vers

À gauche du paysage l'écriteau: SORTIE

Entre dix heures et minuit
Il y a une mandoline au nord de l'Italie

FILM

Cowboy in the eyes and the Far West
Charms the bird with a gesture
Cowboy of the eye my vehicle
Promise of rivers in the first act
Cowboy who grows at dusk
And wants to leap into the audience intact

He whistles the Niagara and stops its noise
The curtain comes down a much finer cataract
Then on the flower and the beacon that are settling in
There is a sigh that the night makes
And up there Venus pins on a bow-tie

Young girl smiling at the universe
She will be queen of all sea dreams
I love your hat on the prairie
And the shepherd guarding his flock of worms

On the left of the landscape the sign: EXIT

Between ten p.m. and midnight
There is a mandolin in northern Italy

LA MATELOTE

Matelot conduisant les vagues au port d'été
À chaque pas de chaleur la lune nous gifle
Et la mer se défait
Agitée par le vent des pêcheurs qui sifflent

    L'océan est vert de tant d'espoir noyé

Les bateaux traînent les vagues jusqu'à monter au ciel
Ils vont charger l'aurore éventuelle
Tels que les escarpins ils aiment l'horizon
L'horizon en arc raide pour la chanson et pour la flèche
Chemin de la colombe en dépêche

        Mon œil mieux qu'un navire divague
        Bien que je sois le marin précis
            Que voulez-vous

La mer change de vagues
Le caméléon de couleur
Et la montre d'heure

Mais l'océan transitoire en échelle sans tapis
Au fond change aussi peu que le charbon des mines
Et je l'aime comme une bouteille ou un bouquet poli
A l'ombre de son phare qui moud les vagues en sourdine

L'océan l'océan le phare et la farine
Pleure mon beau marin sur la marine

L'océan l'océan
        Voilà mon seul drapeau

THE HORNPIPE

Sailor leading the waves to the summer port
With each step in the heat the moon slaps us
And the sea breaks free
Shaken by the wind from fishermen whistling

    The ocean is green with so much drowned hope

Boats drag the waves right up to the sky
They're going to load the coming dawn
Just like court shoes they love the horizon
The horizon steeply curved for songs and for arrows
A path for the hastening dove

        My eye wanders better than a ship
        Although I am the meticulous sailor
            What do you want

The sea changes waves
Chameleons change colour
And clocks change time

But the transient ocean on an uncarpeted stairway
In essence unchanging as coal from the mines
And I love it like a bottle or a polished bouquet
In the shade of its lighthouse that grinds the waves in silence

Ocean ocean lighthouse and flour
Weep my fine sailor for the sail

Ocean ocean
        This is my only flag

Chiffonné de bateaux
Déchiré dans les plages
Mon drapeau naturel est troué de naufrages

Creased by boats
Torn on beaches
My native flag is holed through with wrecks

YA VAS HATCHOU

J'ai été partout et nulle part comme un air de musique

J'ai vu l'amour et le cheval antique
Les vagues de la mer mourant de peste
Le train la vie le pleur qui résoud son théorème

Et niché sur un nuage voyageant vers l'Est
Un oiseau qui chantait oublié de lui-même

Au fond je t'aime
Tu es plus pâle que l'heure et tu fais la légende
Tes paupières sont la seule chose qui s'envole
Et tu es bien plus belle que le retour du pôle

Pendant la nuit
Ton cœur luit

Toi seule vis
Dehors c'est la fin du monde et du violoncelle
Une larme tremble au bord du ciel

La terre s'éloigne et se dégonfle
Tels que tes yeux et ta figure

La chambre s'est vidée par la serrure

YA VAS KHACHU

I've been everywhere and nowhere like a musical air

I've seen love and the ancient horse
Ocean waves dying of plague
Train Life Mourning that solves its theorem

And nestled on a cloud travelling eastward
A bird singing forgotten by itself

Deep down I love you
You are paler than time and are the source of legends
Your eyelids are the only things that fly away
And you are far more beautiful than the return from the Pole

During the night
Your heart shines

You alone are alive
Outside it's the end of the world and of the instrument
A tear trembles on the edge of the firmament

The earth moves away and deflates
Just like your eyes and your face

The room has emptied out through the keyhole

The title is a transliteration of the Russian, Я ВАС ХОЧУ [I want you / I desire you].

POÈME

Colonise la douleur avec ta voix
Enfant de mer sans souci alterne
Il dort à l'ombre de ma flûte et de ses doigts

Regarde bien mon cœur est une lanterne
Et mes prières montent comme l'arbre en escalier interne

Je te dis que tu es belle
Comme une chambre d'hôtel

Tu cherches l'échelle de corde et le violon civil
Ici sous l'églantine
Et la couronne d'épines
Dis-moi toujours que tu adores mes cils

Si j'étais ruisseau ou bien touriste
Vous m'aimeriez tous comme on aime les artistes
Mais je déteste l'hiver et les draps de l'œil
Et ta petite étoile qui tourne à merveille

J'aime la patience et l'hirondelle
Le lit à voile pour le voyage sans rêve
Quand les vagues rongent la nuit précise
Et la tête monte et le ballon crève
Sous le papier de lune qui s'éloigne et glisse
Cherchant les mots qui pendent au ciel

POEM

Colonise pain with your voice
Carefree child of the sea turns over
He sleeps in the shade of my flute and his fingers

Look closely my heart is a lamp
And my prayers climb the staircase inside like a tree

I tell you you're a belle
Like a room in this hotel

You search for the rope ladder and the polite violin
Here beneath the rosehip
And the crown of thorns
Tell me always you love my lashes

If I were a stream or even a tourist
You would all love me the way artists are loved
But I despise winter and the eye's sheets
And your little star spinning flawlessly

I love patience and swallows
The bed with sails for the dreamless journey
As waves gnaw at the very night
And the head rises and the balloon bursts
Under the paper moon that slides away
Searching for words hanging from the sky

VERSIONS ESPAGNOLES

VERSIONES ESPAÑOLAS

SPANISH VERSIONS

ESTÍO EN SORDINA

El estío de golpe sobre la vereda de enfrente
Del lado de la sombra pasa el viento

Estamos sentados alrededor de una voz
En tu dedo se posa un pájaro de color
Mientras que los duraznos sordamente se hinchan

El pájaro picotea las nubes
En que viajan las lluvias silenciosas

Vendimia de los meses y uvas del día
Por distante que esté el pisadero siempre se llega a él

Y el tropel de las nubes
Sigue lentamente los caminos del aire

En el cielo
          el cielo
                    mi redil

Le grito a la pastora
Haz entrar tu manada de camas de hospital
Es ya muy tarde en tu país natal

Mis días se van
Cierra con llave el horizonte

El horizonte en el horizonte se cansa
Vendimia de los años

                Las nubes van al pisadero
Hay que lavar el cielo porque se ha puesto negro
Demasiado negro demasiado negro demasiado negro

SILENT SUMMER

The summer all of a sudden on the opposite kerb
On the shaded side the wind passes through

We are seated around a voice
A coloured bird perches on your finger
While the peaches swell silently

The bird pecks at the clouds
Where silent rains are travelling

Harvest of months and grapes of day
No matter how far away the wine press is you can still get there

And the flock of clouds
Slowly follows paths in the air

In the sky
           the sky
                      my sheepfold

I cry out to the shepherdess
Bring in your flock of hospital beds
It's already very late in your native land

My days go on their way
Close the horizon lock and key

The horizon on the horizon is getting weary
Harvest of the years

                  The clouds go to the wine press
The sky has to be washed because it has turned black
Too black too black too black

La noche se escapa de mi armario

La noche
        La luna ha atravesado sin hacer ruido

The night escapes from my wardrobe

At night
        The moon passed by without making a sound

TARDE

Yo poseo la llave del otoño
El pecho está llena de alas amarillas
Y lloraré una tarde todos los arroyos

EL DÍA MUERE EN TUS MEJILLAS

Ondula tus cabellos la música del arpa
El mundo viene a dormir bajo estas ramas
Un último recuerdo
Se ha posado en mi dedo

PÁJARO VACÍO

Todas las canciones cayeron en el río

Y aquello que guardaba en mi garganta
Se alejó sobre el alba

EVENING

    I possess the key to Autumn
My chest is full of yellow wings
And one evening I will weep out all the streams

    THE DAY IS DYING IN YOUR CHEEKS

    Harp music puts curls in your hair
The world comes to sleep under these branches
One last memory
Has alighted on my finger

    EMPTY BIRD

    All the songs fell into the river

And the one that remained in my throat
Went away at dawn

CABELLERA

Hay una música silvestre
En tus cabellos leves
    Y la lluvia nocturna
    Bajo el astro sonámbulo
TU CABELLERA LLUEVE SOBRE EL CAMPO
Alguien no encontrará el camino
Y tras del horizonte caerá al vacío
      ESTRELLA NATAL
  Este pájaro en el pecho me hace mal
  Y mi vida
  Se quedó muy atrás medio dormida
Al borde de la tarde
Una voz me decía
SER CIEGO AL MEDIODÍA
    Yo miraba
    Mi techo
      dulce mar de mis andanzas
    Y el collar de tus lágrimas
    Ajado en mi garganta
Humareda del vacío
Cabellera fiel de mi navío
     Esos hilos que suben al confín
     Son apenas tres cuerdas de violín

HAIR

There is a wild music
In your light hair
    And the night-time rain
    Under the sleepwalking star
YOUR HAIR RAINS OVER THE COUNTRYSIDE
Someone will not find their way
And beyond the horizon will fall into space
        NATIVE STAR
   This bird in my chest is hurting me
   And my life
   Remains far behind half-asleep
On the cusp of evening
A voice told me
BEING BLIND AT NOON
     I was watching
     My roof
       placid sea of my adventures
     And the necklace of your tears
     Corroded in my throat
Smoke from the void
Faithful hair from my ship
     These threads rising to the boundary
     Are just three strings from my violin

POEMA FUNERARIO

El pájaro de lujo ha cambiado de estrella
Aparejad bajo la tempestad de las lágrimas
Los velas del ataúd
Donde se aleja el instrumento del encanto

En las vegetaciones de los recuerdos
Las horas en torno nuestro hacen los viajes

    Va de prisa
        Va de prisa impelido por los suspiros
El mar está cargado de naufragios
Y yo he adornado el mar para su paso

Es así el viaje primordial y sin billete
El viaje instructivo et secreto
En los corredores del viento

Las nubes se separan para que él pueda pasar
Y las estrellas se iluminan para mostrar el camino

¿Qué buscas en los bolsillos de tu casaca
Has perdido la llave?

En medio de ese zumbido celeste
Encuentras en todas partes tus horas envejecidas
El viento es negro y hay estalactitas en mi voz

Dime Guillermo
Has perdido la llave del infinito

Una estrella impaciente iba a decir que tiene frío

La lluvia afilada empieza a coser la noche

FUNERAL POEM

The luxurious bird has changed stars
Beneath the storm of tears rig
The coffin's sails
Where the enchanted instrument fades away

In the flora of memories
The hours all around us go off on journeys

    It's in a hurry
        It's in a hurry driven by sighs
The sea is laden with wrecks
And I have adorned the sea for its passage

That's how it is the vital but unticketed journey
The informative and secret journey
Along the corridors of the wind

The clouds drift apart so it can pass
And the stars light up to show the way

What are looking for in your jacket pockets
Have you lost your key?

In the midst of this celestial humming
Everywhere you meet your aged hours
The wind is black and there are stalactites in my voice

Tell me Guillaume
Have you lost the key to infinity

An impatient star was about to say it was cold

The sharp rain begins stitching the night

OCÉANO O DANCING

Jazz-band del Océano
Este barco baila mal y yo pierdo el paso
Allá
        El cielo y el mar se juntan
Tanto peor si el cielo es azul y el pez se ahoga

A bordo de la mar se mece el puerto
Por donde voy guardo esta cadencia
Beso tus manos que desanudan los días
Tus manecitas se van siempre
Como los barcos amor cabellera del horizonte

Retrocede el puerto
                      última canción
Mi garganta helada
                tus dedos también

Y a lo lejos alzas tu corazón
Como se alza una flor

Pero el ritmo de tu pecho está en el mar
Y las olas están cálidas del ritmo de tu corazón

Amor amor del joven nadador
Que toca el arpa entre las olas
                      El horizonte se deshace
Espuma que nace
            espuma que muere
Espuma qui danza entre las horas

El mar está fatigado de agitar sus pañuelos
A los navíos que se alejan

OCEAN OR DANCING

Jazz band of the Ocean
This boat dances badly and I miss my step
Over there
              The sky and the sea come together
Too bad if the sky is blue and the fish is drowning

Aboard the sea the port is swaying
Everywhere I go I keep up this pace
I kiss your hands that unravel the days
Your little hands always leave
Like boats like love like the horizon's hair

The port retreats
                      final song
My throat frozen
                      your fingers too

And far away you raise up your heart
As if raising a flower

But the rhythm of your breast is in the sea
And the waves are warm with the rhythm of your heart

Love love of the young swimmer
Playing the harp amongst the waves
                              The horizon is falling apart
Sea foam being born
                    sea foam dying
Sea foam dancing amongst the hours

The sea is weary of waving its handkerchiefs
At departing ships

La noche habitual cumple su deber
Luna taza de leche
                    Nuestras estrellas se cuidan
El océano del sur entre dos árboles
Muchas coronas en el agua
El bien querido océano bajo el mármol

Beberás gota a gota el claro de luna cálido
Esta humareda que sube de las olas
Arrastra lentamente su barco
Poema de la tarde juguete de niño

Los navíos se alejan como tus manos

The usual night does its duty
Moon cup of milk
                         Our stars take care of themselves
The southern ocean between two trees
Many crowns in the water
The beloved ocean beneath the marble

Drop by drop you will drink the hot moonlight
This smoke rising from the waves
Slowly drags its boat along
Evening poem child's toy

Ships move away like your hands

TOUT À COUP

(1922-1923)

ALL OF A SUDDEN

(1922-1923)

1

Les deux ou trois charmes des escaliers du hasard sont incontestables
Tout est calme derrière les miaulements externes   Là-haut
Montez vers l'avenir précis où les vagues du ciel caressent les sables
Mais il y a quand même dans les surprises de l'eau
Quelques îles semées par les explorateurs qui nous devancent

Une certaine chaleur s'échappe des plis des drapeaux secoués
                                                                     [par le vent

De mât en mât les mots se balancent
Et un oiseau mange les fruits du levant

1

The two or three charms of the stairways of chance are indisputable
Everything is quiet behind the mewing outside   Up there
Climb towards the very future where the sky's waves caress the sands
But in the surprises of water there are still
Some islands seeded by explorers who went before us

Some heat escapes from the folds of flags flapping in the wind

From mast to mast the words sway
And a bird eats fruits from the Orient

2

Sur le miroir une araignée qui rame comme une barque régulière
Vers les chanson du marécage
Elle chatouille les souvenirs à la surface et les gestes derrière
Au milieu du silence la mer naufrage

A l'heure des hirondelles
Dieu que les femmes sont belles
Ta femme à les cheveux blonds neufs
Ses yeux sont des jaunes d'œuf
Les yeux des brunes
Sont des jaunes de lune

Parmi les eaux sans musique
Les regards satellites
Se promènent sous les arbres de l'orbite

2

On the mirror a spider rowing like an ordinary boat
Towards the songs of the swamp
It tickles memories up to the surface and leaves gestures behind
Amidst the silence the sea is foundering

In the time of swallows
God how beautiful women are
Your wife has newly blonde hair
Her eyes are like egg yolks
The eyes of brunettes
Are moon yellow

Amongst waters with no music
Satellite glances
Stroll under orbiting trees

3

Je m'éloigne en silence comme un ruban de soie
Promeneur de ruisseaux
Tous les jours je me noie
Au milieu des plantations de prières
Les cathédrales de mes tendresses chantent la nuit sous l'eau
Et ces chants font les îles de la mer

Je suis le promeneur
Le promeneur qui ressemble aux quatre saisons
Le bel oiseau navigateur
Était comme une horloge entourée de coton
Avant de s'envoler m'a dit ton nom

L'horizon colonial est tout couvert de draperies
Allons dormir sous l'arbre pareil à la pluie

3

I go off in silence like a silk ribbon
Walking by streams
Every day I drown
Amidst the prayer plantations
The cathedrals of my affections sing by night underwater
And these songs make islands in the sea

I am the walker
The walker resembling the four seasons
The fine sea bird
Was like a clock wrapped in cotton
Before flying away it told me your name

The colonial horizon is all decked with drapery
Let's go and sleep under the tree that's just like rain

4

Tu n'as jamais connu l'arbre de la tendresse d'où j'extrais mon essence
Il pousse à chaque étage sans préférence
Au milieu d'une discussion de pianos
Il est aussi joli que soixante mètres d'eau

Les yeux de circonstance
Regardent le temps troué
À coups de pistolet

Mais s'il n'y a pas d'oreille
Nos yeux pourtant sont des bouteilles
Vidées à chaque regard
La nuit gardons les yeux dans mon hangar

Maladie d'instrument écoutez son conseil
L'archet glisse glisse sur les escaliers du sommeil
Maladie mélodie
                Cherche bien sous les chaises
Cherche bien sous les ponts
Il y a des morceaux d'âme sciés par mon violon

4

You never knew the tree of tenderness from which I drew my essence
It grows on each floor having no preference
In the midst of a discussion on pianos
It's as pretty as sixty metres of water

The eyes of circumstance
Watch time punctured
By pistol shots

But even if there is no ear
Our eyes are still bottles
Emptied with each glance
At night let's keep our eyes in my hangar

Instrumental malady listen to its advice
The bow slides slides down the sleeping stairs
Malady melody
                    Search hard under the chairs
Search hard under the bridges
There are pieces of soul sawn off by my violin

5

Assis à la limite des sons
Que disait-il du scaphandrier du roi
C'était un lac comme un bonbon
Où fleurissait l'arbre de la foi

Il y a trop de choses qu'on n'a pas vues

Trois jours plongés dans ma mémoire
Il ramène tous les Césars perdus
Le la bémol des belles histoires
Joué dans la harpe d'anciennes pluies
Nous montrent à peine ce qui luit

Plonge plonge royal scaphandrier
Écarte comme des bouteilles les braves grenadiers
Et apporte-moi la corbeille des regards prisonniers

5

Seated at the limit of sound
What was he saying about the king's diver
It was a lake like a piece of candy
Where the faith tree was in flower

There are too many things that haven't been seen

Three days submerged in my memory
He brings back all the lost Caesars
The A-flat of beautiful stories
Played on the harp of ancient rains
Barely show us what's shimmering

Plunge in plunge in royal diver
Discard the brave grenadiers like bottles
And bring me the basket of imprisoned gazes

6

Cinq papillons s'envolent en disant ces prières
Aimez-vous les prières dans la prairie
L'aurore fragile sans étoiles régulières
Pourraient bien se casser à la sortie

Dans le ciel traversent de jolis ruisseaux
Seigneur dis-nous qui a bu le bleu du ciel
Les papillons s'envolent comme des vitraux

Je n'ai pas de chapeau
Et pas d'ombrelle
J'attends toujours une auréole fidèle

6

Five butterflies fly away while saying these prayers
Do you like prayers in the meadow
The fragile dawn without the usual stars
Could well be broken as it leaves

In the sky some pretty rivers flow
Lord tell us who drank the blue from the sky
Butterflies fly away like stained-glass windows

I don't have a hat
Nor an umbrella
I am waiting for a real halo

7

Tu es seulement lézard ou lumière cultivée
Tu as la saveur d'un bon conseil
Et une barbe longue comme l'électricité

Quand ton âme remonte à tes oreilles
Regarder l'extérieur comme un poisson aimé
Tu produis un bon effet

Notre reine est une merveille
Elle a plus de prestige que les sonnets
Elle mange du miel et boit du lait
Miel de silence dans les corbeilles
Tissées par les regards des promeneurs du quai

Chantez le miel poètes chantez
Le miel qui a fait célèbres les abeilles

7

You are only lizard or cultivated light
You have the taste of good advice
And a beard that's long like electricity

When your soul goes back up to your eyes
Examine the outside like a beloved fish
You have a good effect

Our queen is a marvel
She has more prestige than sonnets
She eats honey and drinks milk
Honey of silence in baskets
Woven with the glances of walkers on the quay

Sing of honey poets let's name
The honey that brought the bees fame

8

Maintenant écoutez le grincement des paupières
C'est à cause du vent qu'elles se ferment à grand bruit
À cette heure justement nous sortons d'ordinaire
Et je regarde à travers la passoire des pluies
Sur mes côtes natales décharger les rivières

Il est beau le paysage amical enfermé dans les yeux
A l'instant où je coupe des morceaux d'ennui
Dans les formations des sentiments brumeux
Tu es aussi méritoire que la pluie

8

Now listen to the eyelids creaking
It's because of the wind that they close with a loud noise
At this very hour we usually go out
And I look through the colander of rain
Dumping rivers onto my native shores

It's beautiful the friendly landscape locked in your eyes
At the moment when I cut boredom from a skein
Into formations of misty desires
You are as worthy as the rain

9

Dans une soirée d'épaules de luxe
Un éventail plus joli que la lune
Madame fait le croissant à volonté
Elle est la reine des vagues communes
Elle conduit les vents et les marées

À l'heure de la sortie
La mer du nord sent les grains d'anis
Sur les vagues en retard éclate une discussion
Quand le thermomètre de l'aurore monte à l'horizon

Alors je m'éloigne très atlantique
Sans besoin de prendre le transatlantique
Sur les ondes en sandales de la musique

Son lit loin de la fête polaire et de la mer docile
Elle rêve couchée comme un poisson tranquille

9

At a reception for luxurious shoulders
A fan prettier than the moon
Madame makes the croissant to order
She is the queen of shared waves
She drives the winds and the tides

At the hour of departure
The northern sea smells like aniseed
On the overdue waves an argument breaks out
When the dawn's thermometer climbs to the horizon

So I am moving far away very atlantic
Without needing to take the transatlantic
On the sandalled waves of music

Its bed far from the polar festival and the docile sea
It dreams reclining like a motionless fish

10

Elle disait des phrases rondes comme des bagues
Elle répétait le discours des vagues
Elle parlait parlait

Sors mon petit violoncelle
Sors ma lune bien-aimée
Sors te promener
Comme un aveugle ou comme une épée

Monte jusqu'au dernier étage
Alors elle pourra dire à mes amis
Connais-tu le pays
Je connais le pays

Elle nous dira tout bas comme une abeille sincère
Les racontars astronomiques de l'univers
Avec un bon goût de coquillage
Petit gramophone des plages
Qui garde jaloux les secrets de la mer

Elle pourra dire à mes amis
Messieurs la lune se décolle
J'ai compté toutes les monnaies de l'infini
La rose qui manque au pôle
                              Là voici

10

She uttered phrases round as rings
She repeated the words of the waves
She talked and talked

Come out my little cello
Come out my beloved moon
Come out for a stroll
Like a blind man or like a sword

Go up to the top floor
Then she can say to my friends
Do you know the country
I know the country

Softly like a sincere bee she'll tell us
Astronomical tales of the universe
With a nice taste of shellfish
Small gramophone for beaches
That jealously keeps the secrets of the sea

She can tell my friends
Gentlemen the moon is being peeled away
I have counted all the coins of infinity
The rose that's missing at the pole
                                        Here it is

11

Je suis un peu lune et commis voyageur
J'ai la spécialité de trouver les heures
Qui ont perdu leur montre

Croyez-moi bien
Sous mon œil d'amiral tout se rencontre
Et ce n'est pas plus rare que les cas d'enfants
Perdus dans les magasins

Il y a des heures qui se noient
Il y en a d'autres mangées par les cannibales
Je connais un oiseau qui les boit
On peut les faire aussi mélodies commerciales

Mais dans les bals atlantiques ainsi déguisées
C'est très difficile de les distinguer

11

I'm a bit of a moon and a travelling salesman
I specialise in finding hours
That have lost their watch

You should believe me
Under my admiral's eye it all comes together
And it's no rarer than cases of children
Lost in department stores

There are hours that are drowned
There are others eaten by cannibals
I know a bird that drinks them down
Songs made from them can be commercial

But in the Atlantic balls dressed so smart
It's very hard to tell them apart

12

Sur mon ombrelle en larmes
Petit hirondelle pourquoi pleures-tu

Je connais bien l'alphabet des charmes
Que vous écrivez avec l'encre de vos vertus
Dans les tissus de l'air qui couvre les avenues

Vous savez que la nuit le ciel pointe ses armes
Sur nous
Malheur à celui qui reste debout
Alors vous vous éloignez en riant
Et cela signifie
Que vous laissez la place au camouflage des chauves-souris

Le destin est un ruisseau
Qu'il faut sauter au bon moment
Seigneur il y a un aveugle ami au bord de l'eau
Les hirondelles de mon destin
Fouillent les coins du ciel en souriant

12

On my umbrella in tears
Little swallow why do you weep

I know well the alphabet of charms
That you write with the ink from your virtues
In the fabric of air that covers the avenues

You know at night the sky points its weapons
Right at us
Woe to him who stands still
So you move away laughing
And that means
You give way to the camouflage of bats

Fate is a stream
That must be jumped at the right moment
Lord there's a blind friend by the water's edge
The swallows of my fate
Scour the corners of the sky with a smile

13

Au bord intact du silence absolument humanisé
Je chauffe mes mélodies et mes pieds
Tout est la même chose avec la différence
D'un petit paradis offert à outrance

Vous perdez votre temps orpheline pour tempête oubliée
Lentement les larmes descendent l'escalier
Les larmes sont les plaisirs des télescopes et d'instruments à vent
Quand battent les colombes des applaudissements
Et l'émotion ondule sur les artères du vent

13

At the solid edge of the totally humanised silence
I warm my songs and my feet
Everything's just the same with one difference
From a little paradise offered to excess

You're wasting your orphaned time for a forgotten storm
Slowly tears come down the staircase
Tears are the joys of telescopes and wind instruments
When doves beat their applause
And feelings ripple through the wind's arteries

14

Tombe tombe
Avalanche des solitudes
Sur les vacances de mes yeux

Les regards de l'inquiétude
Montent vers les petits oiseaux et les cloches ambulantes

Avalanche intérieure et consciente
Le ciel se déchire comme une colombe

Les yeux migrateurs sont dans l'embarcadère
Attendant le virage de la nuit qui tombe tombe
La nuit qui est riche comme la capitale
Farcit les coins du silence inégal

Brossez sans vent le rideau du jour
Hier au milieu d'une transmutation saisissable
Tristement s'en allèrent les acrobates et l'amour
Vers les rives du regard patauger sur le sable

14

Falling falling
Avalanche of loneliness
On my eyes' holidays

Anxious glances
Rise towards the little birds and itinerant bells

Avalanche internal and deliberate
The sky splits apart like a dove

The migrating eyes are on the pier
Awaiting the turn of night that's falling falling
The night rich as the capital
Stuffs the corners with uneven silence

Brush the day's curtains without any wind
Yesterday amidst a definable transmutation
Sadly acrobats and love walked off
To the shores of the eye wading on the sand

15

Une main se pose sur le silence
Sur le silence plein de bon Dieu
Tout plein des trous du bon Dieu

Entre les rails à toute vitesse la nuit s'avance
Et ma tristesse entre les rails des yeux

Maintenant que fait-elle
A genoux entre deux hirondelles
Ou parmi les rochers des moribonds
Conducteurs de l'électricité vers l'au-delà
Comme un discours profond
Qui se noya

Les rails des belles paroles
Sortent de la bouche de l'orateur
Les passagers sont brillants comme s'ils venaient du pôle
Et ils poussent des cris en branches de douleur

15

A hand alights on the silence
On the silence filled with the good Lord
Completely filled with the holes of the good Lord

Along the rails night advances at full speed
And my sadness along the rails of my eyes

Now what is she doing
On her knees between two swallows
Or amongst the rocks of the dying
Conductors of electricity to the afterlife
Like a profound speech
That drowned

Rails of fine words
Emerge from the orator's mouth
The passengers glitter as if coming from the Pole
And they cry out in branches of pain

16

Tous les aveugles sont assis au pôle
Ils sont d'un blanc blanc
Ils respirent des bouquets d'amertume bénévole
Et ils mangent un rêve inconsistant

Sur la farine des plaines une fleur chante comme un tambour
Tambour de l'horizon à la levée du jour

Le funiculaire du prince mont mieux que le soleil
Il va plus haut que nos pensées premières
Et jette un œuf qui se casse comme un conseil

Chanson de laboureur
Pour l'aveugle qui grimpe du côté de la lune
Il laboure son empire d'amateur

Nous les aveugles nous sommes des dunes
Où filtre le sable des paroles

Au fond de notre tête s'accroche l'échelle de la chanson
Personne n'écarte nos rideaux
Les doigts d'aveugles sont des papillons

16

The blind are all seated at the Pole
They are all white white
They're breathing bouquets of benevolent bitterness
And they're eating an inconsistent dream

On the flour of the plains a flower sings like a drum
Drum from the horizon at daybreak

The prince's funicular climbs better than the sun
It goes higher than our first thoughts
And throws an egg that breaks like piece of advice

Song of the ploughman
For the blind man who climbs up the side of the moon
He's ploughing his amateur empire

We the blind we are dunes
Where sand is filtered from words

At the back of our heads hangs the song's ladder
No one parts our curtains
The fingers of the blind are butterflies

17

Parmi les grandes figues de l'espace
Quelle douleur douloureuse reste assise devant
Le calvaire du couchant

Maman les vitraux du vide se cassent
Comme des grands papillons gazeux

La nuit descend ses escaliers

Montagnard voulez-vous les chaussures du bon Dieu
Et un petit paravent
Voulez-vous un panier
Plein de cerises ou de cheveux du vent
Voulez-vous un oiseau pour les usines
Voulez-vous un sandwich de lumière pour les alpins
Et un orchestre liquide pour les alpines

17

Among the great figs of space
What painful pain stays seated before
The calvary of sunset

Mama the void's stained-glass windows are breaking
Like great sparkling butterflies

The night goes down its stairs

Highlander do you want the shoes of the good Lord
And a small partition
Do you want a basket
Full of cherries or wind-blown hair
Do you want a bird for the factories
Do you want a sandwich of light for the men from the Alps
And a liquid orchestra for the women from the Alps

18

Me voici au bord de l'espace et loin des circonstances
Je m'en vais tendrement comme une lumière
Vers la route des apparences
Je reviendrai m'asseoir sur les genoux de mon père
Un beau printemps rafraîchi par l'éventail des ailes
Quand les poissons déchirent le rideau de la mer
Et le vide est gonflé d'un regard virtuel

Je reviendrai sur les eaux du ciel

J'aime voyager comme le bateau de l'œil
Qui va et vient à chaque clignotement
Six fois déjà j'ai touché le seuil
De l'infini qui renferme le vent

Rien dans la vie
Qu'un cri d'antichambre
Nerveuses océaniques quel malheur nous poursuit
Dans l'urne des fleurs sans patience
Se trouvent les émotions en rythme défini

18

Here I am on the edge of space and out of the loop
I am leaving tenderly like a light
Headed for the road of perceptions
I will return to sit on my father's knee
A beautiful Spring refreshed by the fan of wings
When fish tear the curtain away from the sea
And the void is filled with a virtual gaze

I will return to the waters of heaven

I love to travel like the boat in the eye
Coming and going with each blink
Six times already I've touched the threshold
Of infinity that holds back the wind

Nothing in life
But a cry from the antechamber
Oceanic nerves what misfortune pursues us
In the urn of flowers with no patience
You find emotions in a set rhythm

19

Péripéties d'album sans couchant
Et sans feu à bout portant
Plus tard
Il y a quelques constellations désintéressées
Nous sommes pensifs et le ciel se remplit
Le noyau de la solitude est très bien étudié
Mais le ciel se remplit comme un théâtre populaire

Le ciel est gratuit

Avec ses oiseaux expansifs et ses murs d'air
Il est presque aussi maternel que les drapeaux
Et le soir
Dans ses sillons poussent de grands oiseaux
Qui viennent délicatement nous dire au revoir

19

Adventures from the album with no sunset
And with no fire at close range
Later on
There are some selfless constellations
We are thoughtful and the sky fills up
The core of loneliness has been thoroughly studied
But the sky fills up like a popular theatre

The sky is free of charge

With its effusive birds and its walls of air
It's almost as maternal as the flags
And in the evening
In its furrows grow large birds
That delicately come to say goodbye to us

20

Il y a des lézards sur la vallée des larmes
Plus beaux que les bijoux dans le sommeil des cambrioleurs
Il y a aussi les chameaux de l'espace et des charmes
Chargés d'horizon et d'oasis sans heures

Au milieu de ton regard je vois pousser des fleurs
Et tout au fond un moulin fatigué
Comme le Christ docile aux horoscopes

J'aime regarder
Cette eau mélancolique comme les yeux de Dieu
Qui ne peut pas ressusciter
Il voudrait descendre les marches de la nuit
Tel que les sons des cloches descendent la pluie
Mais il est arrêté par les syncopes
Des destins précis

20

There are lizards in the valley of tears
More beautiful than jewellery in the sleep of thieves
There are camels too from space and charms
Loaded with horizons and timeless oases

In the midst of your gaze I see flowers growing
And at the very end a worn-out mill
Like Christ amenable to horoscopes

I like watching
This melancholy water like the eyes of God
That cannot be resurrected
It would like to go down the stairs of night
Just as the ringing of bells brings down the rain
But it has been stopped by the syncopation
Of definite fates

21

Sa voix monte le long des pluies
Appelant au secours au bord des inconsciences

Ils sont venus cette nuit
Cambrioler le silence
Comme une blanchisserie

Les voyages des somnambules en lumière de finesse
Respirent mes divagations
Quand viennent les poètes avec les fleuves amis
Apporter les coussins de la tendresse
Je mets des souliers neufs à mes chansons

Les voleurs cherchent des pyramides dans les yeux calmes et sans musique
Dans les beaux yeux des dromadaires
Ou dans les spirales d'air
Qui déplacent les danseuses géographiques

21

His voice rises with the rains
Calling for help on the verge of unconsciousness

They came last night
Burgling the silence
Like a laundry room

The journeys of sleepwalkers in a subtle light
Breathe in my ramblings
When poets come with friendly rivers
Bringing pillows of tenderness
I put new shoes on my songs

Thieves look for pyramids in quiet eyes free of music
In the beautiful eyes of camels
Or in spirals of air
That displace geographic dancers

22

Tu veux cueillir les ruisseaux que j'aime
Pour te faire des gants
Quand tu lèves la main
Chargée de calories vers les nuages extrêmes
Tu ressembles au mot SOUDAIN

Là-bas dans le loin loin
Où la mer gratte les pieds du ciel
Une horloge chante avec ardeur
Quel beau voyage dans les yeux de lenteur
En regardant ce ciel d'été
Tellement chargé d'oiseaux qu'il s'est cassé

Le ballon revient dans les plus belles histoires
En rapportant les jours perdus dans sa nacelle
Et la mer chatouille les pieds du ciel
Pour le faire pleuvoir

22

You want to pick the streams I love
To make yourself some gloves
When you raise your hand
Calorie-laden to the extreme clouds
You look like the word SUDDEN

Over there far far away
Where the sea scratches at the sky's feet
A clock sings with passion
What a beautiful journey in sluggish eyes
Looking at this summer sky
So laden with birds that it broke

The balloon returns in the most beautiful stories
Bringing back lost days in its basket
And the sea tickles the sky's feet
To make it rain

23

Noyé charmant quelle heure est-il
Dis-moi la consistance des rêveries
Interchangeables en chaos civil

Le calme est plein de laines de mouton
Et je ne sais rien

Dans les souffrances en marche sur la vie
Les linges sèchent jour et nuit
Sur la corde de l'horizon
(Cela se passe très loin)

Noyé charmant
La belle musique des équinoxes entraine les amants
Selon la loi des gravitations
Et déteint les murs du salon

Noyé charmant
Si tu voyais maintenant
Les vagues apprivoisées
Venir avec des révérences à nos pieds

Noyé charmant
Que t'a dit la Sainte Vierge
Carde-t-elle encore la rose des vents
Entre ses doigts diaphanes
Que discutent les autres saints
Dans leur langage d'aéroplane

23

Nice drowned man what time is it
Tell me of the consistency of daydreams
Interchangeable in civil chaos

The calm is full of sheep's wool
And I know nothing

In suffering on the move through life
Laundry dries day and night
On the line of the horizon
(That happens very far away)

Nice drowned man
The beautiful equinoctial music leads lovers
According to the law of gravity
And fades the walls of the living room

Nice drowned man
If now you could see
The domesticated waves
Coming reverently to our feet

Nice drowned man
What did the Blessed Virgin tell you
Does she still card the compass rose
Between her diaphanous fingers
What do the other saints talk about
In their aeroplane language

24

Je connais les chemins dociles
Qui relient nos douleurs dans l'atmosphère
Et la voiture des battements homogènes
Qui va et vient sous le réverbère

Tu es lumière et ruisseau de l'est à l'ouest
Tu caches des souvenirs
Dans les poches de ta veste
Et tu penses une étoile filante

Aujourd'hui penché au bord de moi-même
J'éparpille mes rêves ambulants
En évasions multiples sans retard
Mais le miroir se tient très calme
Pour les naufrages des regards

Les plus précieux de ta mémoire
S'éloignent maintenant au fil de l'eau
Ma tendresse pense une étoile filante
Qui viendrait se poser comme un oiseau

24

I know the meek paths
That connect our sorrows in the atmosphere
And the car thumping consistently
That comes and goes under the lamp post

You are light and a stream running east to west
You hide memories
In your jacket pockets
And you think of a shooting star

Today leaning at my side
I scatter my pipedreams
In multiple escapes with no delay
But the mirror keeps very calm
For foundering glances

The most precious of all in your memory
Now floating away downstream
My tenderness thinks of a shooting star
That would come and perch like a bird

25

Il revient à la nage des aurores précédentes
À la nage au contour de la musique
Et le piano accroît les lunes conscientes
À l'heure du télescope et des prières antiques

Les oiseaux faits à l'enclume
S'envolent vers d'autres cieux faire leurs éloges
Donnerez-vous aux tonnerres vos édredons de plumes
Les heures mûrissent dans les horloges
Jetez-nous les monnaies de vos gosiers
Que j'apprenne à tendre des ponts entre les nuages
Que j'apprenne à suivre le tunnel du sang
Et que je connaisse le marteau de l'âge
Et l'entrepreneur des émotions sortantes
Sortantes demain

25

He's swimming back from previous dawns
Swimming to the pattern of the music
And the piano increases the conscious moons
When it's time for the telescope and ancient prayers

Birds fashioned on an anvil
Fly away to other skies to give them praise
Will you thunder out your feather quilts
The hours are maturing in clocks
Throw us coins from your gullets
So I can learn to build bridges between the clouds
So I can learn to follow the tunnel of blood
And so I can know the hammer of the age
And the contractor of emotions that are going out
Going out tomorrow

26

Regarde l'arc-en-ciel et l'acrobate
L'acrobate qui saute sur le vertige des mots
Il est beau comme un ange qui s'acclimate
Prendra-t-il les habitudes de mes oiseaux

Regarde le cristal qui pousse en fleur éblouie
Regarde la ruche bouillante de mon cerveau
L'arc-en-ciel honorable en tissus de drapeau

L'arc-en-ciel verse sa musique antagoniste
Sur le fleuve qui partage la nuit
Regarde cette lune extra pour les touristes

La belle machine sentimentale
Et la colombe rotative qui élargit l'espace
Toujours égale

Regarde le médium nerveux de la lumière
Conduisant les sentiers qui perdent l'espoir
Regarde l'horizon qui se ferme après les missionnaires

Regarde ton regard
Et le fond de mon cœur où il fait un peu tard
Tu sais
Je vole au ras de terre quand il va pleuvoir

26

Look at the rainbow and the acrobat
The acrobat jumping over the vertigo of words
He's handsome as an angel who has settled in
Will he adopt the customs of my birds

Look at the crystal growing into a dazzling flower
Look at the boiling hive of my brain
The honourable rainbow made of flag cloth

The rainbow pours its antagonistic music
Onto the river that divides the night
Look at this moon made especially for tourists

The beautiful sentimental machine
And the rotating dove that expands space
Always the same

Look at the nervous medium of light
Leading paths that are losing hope
Look at the horizon which is closing after the missionaries

Gaze at your gaze
And deep in my heart where it's a little late
You know
I fly at ground level when it's going to rain

27

Moulin à vent sur la prairie
Moulin moulin prenez garde aux aveugles
Qu'as-tu donc aujourd'hui
Moulin de ma conscience comme il est loin notre pays

Les barques voguent sur la lumière surélevée
Semblables aux mots des poètes aimés
Ou bien aux éventails de la saison
Sur le chemin de l'adieu normal

Petits palmiers de la frontière des diapasons
Tous les aveugles ont des aimants aux doigts
À cause des pressentiments de douleur végétale

Quand les dieux intimes approchent sans combat
Le moulin du cœur va trop vite

Meunier meunier
Ta belle sourit ses blancheurs oubliés
Ta belle sourit et puis nous quitte

27

Windmill in the pasture
Mill mill beware of blind men
What is it about you today
Mill of my conscience how far away our country is

Boats sail on raised light
A little like the words of favourite poets
Or even seasonal fans
On the way from a normal farewell

Small palm trees on the border with tuning forks
The blind all have magnets on their fingers
Because of premonitions of herbal pain

When the intimate gods approach without a fight
The heart's mill turns too quickly

Miller miller
Your beautiful girl smiles her forgotten whiteness
Your beautiful girl smiles and then leaves us

28

Apportez des jeux
De petites distractions pour l'infini
Qui baille dans le regard de Dieu

Et pile et face
                et jour et nuit

Le ciel traverse lent lent traîné par des gros nuages

Irons-nous surveiller les antipodes
Le ciel commence à avoir de l'âge
Et l'expérience dit
Il faut se soulager en pluie
Ou chercher d'autres amusements

Mais le jour se tourne de l'autre côté
Et c'est l'obscurité

Laissons les parachutes à mi-chemin
Les histoires se dispersent tous les soirs
Quand pousse la rose de l'au-revoir

28

Bring games
Small distractions for infinity
Which yawns under the gaze of God

And heads or tails
                        day or night

The sky crosses slowly slowly dragged by great clouds

Are we going to keep an eye on the antipodes
The sky is beginning to get old
And experience says
You have to relieve yourself in the rain
Or seek other entertainment

But the day turns to the other side
And that's darkness

Let's leave the parachutes halfway
Stories scatter every evening
When grows the farewell rose

29

La nuit comme un ballon descend du ciel
Comme un ballon plein de voyageurs inouïs

Une mandoline joue sur l'univers
Ses émotions démontables qui font des plis
Dans les couches superposées de l'atmosphère

Que tu sois tisserand de pluies
Ou bien fleur d'automobile oubliée
Nous sommes quand même de bons amis
Unis par la chaîne interne des douleurs parallèles

Chante avec nous l'album d'échos ou le missel
Et après sors de ton âme en chaleur d'antan
Les prières et les rubans d'effluves sensuels
Ton âme est ventriloque comme les volcans

29

The night like a balloon comes down from the sky
Like a balloon full of uncanny travellers

A mandolin plays on the universe
Its removable emotions making folds
In the superimposed layers of the atmosphere

Whether you are a weaver of rains
Or even a forgotten automobile flower
We are good friends all the same
United by the internal chain of parallel sorrows

Sing with us the album of echoes or the missal
And then come out of your soul in the heat of yesteryear
Prayers and ribbons with sensual scents
Your soul is a ventriloquist like the volcanoes

30

Madame il y a trop d'oiseaux
Dans votre piano
Qui attire l'automne sur une forêt
Épaisse de nerfs palpitants et des libellules

Les arbres en arpèges insoupçonnés
Perdent parfois l'orientation du globe

Madame je supporte tout   Sans chloroforme
Je descends au fond de l'aube
Le rossignol roi de septembre m'informe
Que la nuit se laisse tomber entre la pluie
Trompant la vigilance de vos regards
Et qu'une voix chante loin de la vie
Pour soutenir l'espace décloué
L'espace si lourd d'étoiles qu'il va tomber

Madame dix heures sent le tabac d'artiste
Vous aimez le nadir au corps d'oiseau
Vous êtes un phénomène léger
Je m'en vais tout seul au couchant des touristes
C'est bien plus beau

30

Madam there are too many birds
In your piano
Which attracts Autumn onto a forest
Thick with excited nerves and dragonflies

Trees in unsuspected arpeggios
Sometimes lose their global orientation

Madam I can handle anything   Without chloroform
I go down into the depths of dawn
The nightingale king of September informs me
That night is falling amongst the rain
Cheating the vigilance of your gaze
And that a voice sings far from life
To support the detached space
Space so heavy with stars that it's going to fall

Madam ten o'clock smells of artist's tobacco
You love the nadir with the body of a bird
You are a gentle phenomenon
I'll go off on my own to the sunset of tourists
It's much nicer that way

31

La belle conduite du calvaire
Mérite un crépuscule de premier ordre
Une mer calme comme un regard de fleur
Où l'eau soit douce à la caresse intime

Rien de déchirures sur les draps des cieux
Et pour réchauffer les pieds
La route des chevelures jusqu'au bord de la terre
Et la vapeur des yeux

Jésus Jésus
tes yeux étaient grands comme deux soldats
Tu auras un bouquet de fleurs
Pour mettre dans ton cœur
Dans ton cœur visible à tous venants
Comme une poche sur la tunique

Tu auras une boîte de chocolat

Je t'aime debout sur la fumée des prières
Je t'aime couché sur les ingratitudes
Je t'aime assis sur les rochers du ciel

Tu auras la Légion d'Honneur

31

The fine conduct of Calvary
Deserves a first-class twilight
A sea calm as a flower's gaze
Where the water is soft to an intimate caress

No rips in the heavens' sheets
And to warm the feet
The road from the hair to the edge of the earth
And steam from the eyes

Jesus Jesus
thine eyes were big as two soldiers
Thou wilt have a bouquet of flowers
To place in thy heart
In thy heart visible to all who come
Like a pocket on thy tunic

Thou wilt have a box of chocolates

I love thee standing above the smoke of prayers
I love thee lying on ingratitude
I love thee sitting on the sky's rocks

Thou wilt have the Legion of Honour

32

Sur le chemin de gauche la saison fuit
Les pigeons dévalent le silence en petits morceaux
Pourquoi ton cœur fait trop de bruit
C'est l'heure où les poissons attentifs comme des fruits de patience
Écoutent descendre le temps au fond de l'eau

Notre vie est parfumée par la distance
Et je suis parallèle parmi les feuilles intégrales
Sur cette campagne au gosier de colombe
Je mange la même nourriture de doléances

Mes colombes s'évanouissent d'émotion spéciale
Le matin calculé de l'harmonium sincère
Lève les regard vers les plus planètes
Le créateur des rayons visuels et de l'époque tertiaire
Qui a la langue en fer rouge comme les prophètes

32

On the path to the left the season flees
Pigeons hurtle through the silence in small pieces
Why does your heart make so much noise
This is the time when fish attentive as the fruits of patience
Listen to time sinking into the water's depths

Our life is perfumed by distance
And I lie parallel amongst perfect leaves
On this countryside with the throat of a dove
I eat the same grievance food

My doves faint out of special feelings
The morning calculated by the sincere harmonium
Raise your eyes to far-off planets
The creator of visual rays and the tertiary era
Who has a tongue of red iron like the prophets

VERSIONS ESPAGNOLES

VERSIONES ESPAÑOLAS

SPANISH VERSIONS

15

Una mano se apoya en el silencio
En el silencio lleno de buen Dios
Totalmente lleno de agujeros de buen Dios

Entre los railes a toda velocidad la noche se acerca
Y mi tristeza entre los railes de los ojos

Qué hace ahora ella
De rodillas entre dos golondrinas
O en medio de las rocas de los moribundos
Conductores de la electricidad hacia el más allá
Como un discurso profundo
Acabado de ahogar

Los railes de las hermosas palabras
Salen de la boca del orador
Los pasajeros están brillantes como sí vinieran del polo
Y lanzan gritos en ramas de dolor

15

A hand rests on the silence
On the silence filled with the good Lord
Completely filled with the holes of the good Lord

Along the rails night approaches at full speed
And my sadness along the rails of my eyes

Now what is she doing
On her knees between two swallows
Or amongst the rocks of the dying
Conductors of electricity to the hereafter
Like a profound speech
That ended up drowning

The rails of fine words
Emerge from the orator's mouth
The passengers are shining as if coming from the Pole
And they cry out in branches of pain

22

Quieres coger los arroyos que me gustan
Para hacerte guantes
Cuando alzas la mano
Cargada de calorías hacia las nubes extremas
Te pareces a la palabra SÚBITO

Allá en la lejanía
Donde el mar araña los pies del cielo
Un reloj canta con ardor
Qué hermoso viaje en los ojos de lentitud
Al mirar este cielo de estío
Que tan cargado de pájaros se ha roto
El globo vuelve en los más bellos cuentos
Trayendo los días perdidos en su barquilla
Y el mar golpea les pies del cielo
Para hacerlo llover

22

You want to pick the streams I like
To make yourself some gloves
When you raise your hand
Calorie-laden to the farthest clouds
You look like the word SUDDEN

Over there in the distance
Where the sea scratches at the sky's feet
A clock sings with passion
What a beautiful journey in the eyes of slowness
Looking at this summer sky
So laden with birds that it is broken
The balloon returns in the most beautiful stories
Carrying lost days in its basket
And the sea tickles the sky's feet
To make it rain

NOTES ON THE TEXT

Automne régulier

The text as printed here follows the first edition wherever possible, but checked against the author's *Obra poética*, 2003 [Poetic Works, henceforward OP]. I have adopted OP's corrections of typographical errors, and the elimination of punctuation, but have followed the first edition in terms of lineation and stanza breaks, as OP offers no rationale for its changes to the latter and is clearly wrong throughout in terms of line breaks. In cases of doubt, I have also consulted *Obras poéticas en francés* [Poetic Works in French; henceforward OPF], ed. Waldo Rojas, (Santiago: Editorial Universitaria, 1998), which is likewise beset with a number of errors. Where there is no clear solution supported by other sources, I have used my own best judgement. To demonstrate the editorial path taken, here below is page 10 of the first edition, showing the beginning of the poem, 'Hiver à boire', the second poem in the book. It is obvious from the first edition's layout that the lines carried over have only been thus treated because the page was not wide enough. The first stanza should therefore be a quatrain with a capital letter starting each line.

HIVER A BOIRE

L'hiver est arrivé à l'appel de quelqu'un
Et les regards émigrent vers les chaleurs connues
Ce soir le vent traîne ses écharpes de vent
Tissez mes oiseaux chéris un toit de chants sur les avenues

Entendez-vous pétiller l'arc-en-ciel mouillé
Sous le poids des oiseaux il s'est plié

L'amertume a peur des intempéries
Mais il nous reste un peu de cendre du couchant
Hirondelles de ma poitrine comme vous faites mal
Secouant toujours ce silence végétal

Eleven of the poems collected in *Automne régulier* had been published previously. Five had already appeared in Huidobro's selected volume, *Saisons choisies* in 1921: 'Automne régulier', 'Femme', 'Globe Trotter', 'Ombres chinoises', and 'Océan ou dancing'. Other prior publications were:

'Automne régulier' (*a fragment only*) in *Action*, Paris, August 1922, and in *Claridad*, Santiago, July 1924.
'Relativité du printemps' in *Paris Journal*, Paris, December 1924.
'Été en sourdine' in *Ariel*, Santiago, June 1925.
'Femme' in *La Vie des lettres*, Paris, 1920.
'Globe-Trotter' in *La Bataille littéraire*, 2:10, Paris, December 1920.
'Film' in *Création*, 3, Paris, February 1924, and in *La Nación*, Santiago, July 1924.
'La Matelote' in *Le Manomètre* (Lyon, February 1924), and in *Universitario*, Paris, November 1924.
'Ya vas hatchou' in *Gargoyle* (Paris, August 1922) and in *Het Overzicht* (Antwerp, April 1924).
'Poème' appeared in the programme of the Grand Bal des Artistes Travesti-Transmental (Paris, 23 Feb., 1923), a legendary event in the avant-garde community in Paris, organised by the expatriate Russian artists resident there.

The Spanish versions printed here first appeared as follows:

'Estío en sordina' in the anthology, *Índice de la nueva poesía americana* [Index of the New American Poetry], edited by Vicente Huidobro & Jorge Luis Borges, Buenos Aires & Mexico City: Sociedad de Publicaciones El Inca, 1926. *NB. The text of this poem in OP contains two clear errors, and I have therefore followed the version printed in* Índice.
'Tarde', a version of 'Clef des saisons', appeared in *Grecia* (Madrid, June 1920)
'Cabellera', a version of 'Affiche', appeared in *Centauro*, 1:1 (Huelva, Nov. 1920) and *Tableros*, 1 (Madrid, 15 Nov. 1921)
'Poema funerario' in *La Opinión*, Santiago, 23 August 1934.
'Océano o dancing' in the same *Índice*, as above.

Tout à coup

The layout here is based upon the 1925 first edition; the only authoritative alternatives are the texts contained in OP, and the earlier OPF. As in some other cases in the largely excellent OP edition, line-endings have been misread, with endings that were forced by the right margin in the first edition being wrongly interpreted as hard endings. The first edition does not help by leaving carried-over text flush with the left margin, but the author's use of initial capitalisation and end-rhyme do make it clear where the lines should begin and end. To demonstrate the editorial decision that I have adopted, here below is Poem 1 from the first edition.

1

Les deux ou trois charmes des escaliers du hasard sont incontestables
Tout est calme derrière les miaulements externes. Là-haut
Montez vers l'avenir précis où les vagues du ciel caressent les sables
Mais il y a quand même dans les surprises de l'eau
Quelques îles semées par les explorateurs qui nous devancent

Une certaine chaleur s'échappe du pli des drapeaux secoués par le vent

De mât en mât les mots se balancent
Et un oiseau mange les fruits du levant

As with the example from *Automne régulier*, the first stanza is a quatrain, but it is clear throughout the book that it is the author's practice to start each line with a capital letter. In addition, line-endings are rendered obvious by the rhyme-scheme. Accordingly, we have printed this as a five-line stanza. The only variation lies with the second line (or fourth in first edition), where we have increased the space before the capitalised "Là-haut", after the elimination of the punctuation mark. I suspect in fact that the whole poem should run in two quatrains, the second one starting with the last line of the current first stanza, giving us – as in the first four lines – an ABAB rhyme-scheme, *devancent / balancent* and *vent / levant*, but there is no independent evidence to support this and I have therefore left things as they are. OP and OPF both follow the layouts of the first edition slavishly, despite using different type-sizes and page-sizes, which I find inexplicable.

The first edition does however contain several typographical errors, which the OP annotates and corrects. However, in Poem 4, OP has conflated two lines, leaving out the last half of one and the first half of another. We assume this to be a transcription error as OP provides no note concerning the variance. In all cases of variant spelling, OP's text has been preferred, and, once again, I have followed OP's guidance as to the elimination of punctuation, the first edition being erratic in this regard. Poem 22 in the Appendix is as printed in OP; Poem 15, however, is the translation, apparently by the author, as printed in *Favorables—París—Poema* Nº 1, in 1926. This is mentioned in OP, but not printed there.

The two Spanish versions printed here first appeared as follows:

Nº 15 in *Favorables—París—Poema* Nº 1, Paris 1926.
Nº 22 in the anthology, *Índice de la nueva poesía americana*, 1926 (details on p. 157).

Tony Frazer
April 2020

www.ingramcontent.com/pod-product-compliance
Lightning Source LLC
Chambersburg PA
CBHW030900170426
43193CB00009BA/680